RECURRENCE

Recurrence

When You Are Caught Between The Dark And The Light

LAUREN REED

Author

Lauren Kamora

Contents

Transpiring

Chapter 1: One Night

There was a door. Inside that door was a dark room with no light. On the outside, the door was shiny and everyone loved that door... until they opened it. When they opened that door, the light from the outside was turned off by the darkness in the room. The room was so dark, some didn't know how anyone could stay in that room. Well, I stuck my head in that room a few times. It was not until one night, I went into that room and shut the door.

One night can change your life forever. One night can determine how you respond to certain things for the rest of your life. When you're young and naive, it is easy to put yourself in a vulnerable situation. This could be showing off your new car, speeding, and crashing it. This could be proving you can do a backflip and breaking your neck... or in this case... it can be indulging in substances and having an unconscious, nonconsensual interaction. The agony may not be apparent immediately, but it will show up. The recollections were never pleasant. I began indulging more and more to get those memories out of my head. When I was under I didn't dream. When I was under I didn't feel. But, when I was under I became so down that I did not care. I tried to trust again, and an acquaintance of the first perpetrator asked for a ride home. Being young and dumb, I fell for it again. That... that was my final straw. I locked that door. No one was allowed in or out.

What about the adjacent door? That door was lit up. I'd had my eye on that door, but never pursued it, because someone was already in the room. Well, that someone left and the door was open. It seemed it was left open for me to stumble across and walk in. So I did. I was in that room having a good time. I didn't realize that soon enough the doors would lead to the same room. Except, on one half of the room was a bright light, and on the other side was pure darkness and fear. Eventually, one half of the room lit up so much the darkness of the other half began to fade away. It's like the sun was beaming through the window. Let's refer to this shining door by name, Guel. Guel and I had an instant connection. It was like we knew each other for years. The daily adventures and memories. The late night talks and the vacations. I was his "girl"... so he said.

The fun was never ending. Emphasis on the *was*. Two months later we had a sudden drift. The doors no longer led to the same room. The doors were in the same building, just on different floors now. They came back together. After a while, the reconnecting and disconnecting became bothersome. The indulging began again. The disputes began. The time disconnected surged. Then, things calmed back down. There was again a lit up room. The light wasn't coming from the sun though. It was a battery operated flashlight that portrayed itself as otherwise. As the batteries died, the room became gloomy and dark. My complaints to Guel about the reoccurring disconnections led to more disputes. Eventually I shut up.

Things were going good. I bought new batteries for the flashlight and mistook it for the sun again. Names were popping up. "Who is she? Who are they?" I had to ask. Was I no longer his "girl?" Had I done something wrong? I'd not dare to ask. I didn't want another disconnect. The disconnect didn't even have to be brought to me. I was checking out. I was ready to turn the light off, since I knew it wasn't real sunlight. It was better to be in a dark room than in one that was lit up by a wannabe sun. By someone who was faking it all. Was it all a lie? Was I just there to fill a void? The light turned off again. But why? Did I ask too many questions? Was this my fault?

I got the flashlight to work again. Until the devil himself walked in the room. Who was that? The perpetrator. I'd known of a preexisting friendship, however I was assured that was over. That was in fact a lie. I did my best to look past this friendship. I did my part of explaining that night the day Guel and I first went out. He knew. You'd think this would influence his decision to continue his friendship with not only my aggressor, but the person who'd double crossed him before as well. For weeks, I let it go. For weeks, I kept quiet. Then... the offender made his remarks against me. Now, it was time to say something. It was time to speak my truth. After contemplating doing such for more than a year, I let it be known what he did.

It was time. It was time to come face to face with the truth. He in fact, did not show up. However, someone else did on his behalf. I had already come to terms and gotten what I had to say ready. The thought of this encounter caused me tons of uneasiness. But I masked it. It was time for me to hold my head high and stop hiding behind this. Maybe this would help me move past it and get some closure. I wasn't looking for an apology, just ownership of his unrighteous actions. Because he decided not to be part of this encounter, though he was the reason I was there, the message was passed along. He did not like this and decided to take revenge. But how could you want revenge on someone you hurt? How could you want to cause someone more pain than you have already put them through? Some questions will never have answers, but I made my own. Truth is, some people are just outright nauseating. One text led to another. The frustration he felt led to his need for revenge. What revenge could he possibly take? Ruining me and Guel. It was over. I didn't feel the same grief I felt before. Why not? Did I really check out months ago when the spark was unplugged? Was I realizing this was God answering my prayers? "God please remove anyone who is doing wrong behind my back. Please remove anyone who does not have good intentions. Please remove anyone that is portraying themselves as someone they are not." I remember that prayer.

Soon after, Guel was gone. But the light was still there. How could that be? He was the light... right? No. He was not. The light was in my room. It was just turned off. He knew this, and brought his flashlight to distract me. I didn't even have to turn the light back on. God did it for me. And that light was SHINING.

Chapter 2: Why?

Why did I ever indulge? Why did I ever pick it up? Could this have been prevented? Those were the questions I asked myself. We cannot live based on "what if I did this?" or "what if I didn't do that?" What's done is done. It is about how we overcome the things we cannot change.

No one forced me in that room and handed me a fix. I was following the wrong light for many years. Not a person, not a thing, but a spirit. The sorrows crept into that room and I tripped at the wrong door. I never knew how to get out of that room. Instead of getting out, I brought things in to temporarily shine light. The spirit did not come in human form. It came in a container. This container changed shapes and sizes through the years. What was in it? Poison. But not the poison you drink and fall to the ground choking on it. The poison you drink that makes you feel better. Is the temporary better worth a prolonged worse? It was time for me to spit the poison out. I tried... but it seemed magnetized to me. But why? Why would I need a fix? What needed fixing? Luxury cars, loving family, nice house, knowledge, beauty, success. Sounds like a pretty good life right? What's not to love? Was that all that it was? Was it that simple? Was there nothing more to ask for? Some might say that describes the perfect life, with no complaints. We must look within to see a problem. Does a pretty door mean a nice, well lit room? No... it does not. The mind is hidden and can only be seen through what is spoken. Not even seen, but heard. Noticed. Recognized. Anyone can throw on a smile like a pair of pants. Does that mean the smile is real? Or is the smile hiding a room of darkness that has yet been discovered? The breakdowns, the heartache, the sorrow seemed continuous. But did it only start that night? Growing up experiencing emotions you cannot describe is a lot for a young child. I was that young child. I was stumbling over these emotions and that... that is how I tripped and fell into that room. I wanted to get out of that room. It was dark and lonely. But if I couldn't get out, I could bring some things in.

Why was I indulging? Let's rewind. Growing up, life was pretty damn good. But there was always something that was off. They don't teach you much about life in school. There I was thinking the light in my room was fading as I got older. Maybe this was part of life. But it didn't fade. It would go off and come back on. Then, it would be off for a while and come back on sometimes, but the majority of the time it was off. That was why... why I began falling off the bed in the dark room. I could not see. I rolled over and on one side was sorrow and on the other side was a fix. Nowhere in that

room were there friends, hanging out, socializing, or any other outlet. I created my own outlet. It was so easy for an innocent mind to get wrapped around a horrible thing. No one closed that door. I was closing my own door without knowing it. The spirits in the room were so strong that when they closed the door, I could not bring myself to open it back up.

Two years later, I was a new me. New school, leveling up. What I did not see were the many challenges I'd face in this new environment. I could no longer spend time indulging. I had to make a choice. These next four years could determine the rest of my life. It was time to focus. Hmmm... could I focus and indulge? Now, I was testing myself to see how far I could roll after falling off the bed in that dark room. Now, on the floor of that room was indulging to be able to keep my head clear, and on the other side was shutting everything out and getting off track. Of course, I never checked the dresser in that room. On that dresser was a hand from God that I should have taken.

At the blink of an eye, two more years went by. It was now the end of the summer. I went to hang out, go to the pool, and have some fun. Then... one night the unimaginable happened. I'd never thought that I'd be left alone in such a state by someone I thought I was cool with, especially by a girl older than me. I thought I'd be looked out for considering others would be joining us. We're listening to music, sippin', and having a good time. Uh oh! Now I'm stumbling. I can't see straight. Maybe I overindulged? Now, he was there. I was out cold. I was listening, but it seemed that my head weighed too much to pick it up off the table. Fast forward a little... I managed to go to the poolside with them. I laid on a pool chair, because standing was no longer an option in my current state. But, I was forcefully accompanied on that chair. That was the night that everything changed.

Although I was already in and out of my recurring indulgence, this caused me to be even more in than out. However I found something worth more than that. I thought I'd found the one. I'd rekindled with a childhood friend. Everything was going so well. We became closer than ever before. I never saw that ending coming... at least not yet. Then one day, I got a call, it was all over. I was thrown to the curb. I spent months trying to figure out why. Losing myself in the process, indulging became my only way to stay sane. I couldn't eat without it, sleep without it, go to school without it... I couldn't do anything.

A few months later, I was open to making more friends. Strictly for a friendship. That is how I ended up letting my guard down, meeting the acquaintance of the perpetrator. Now, nothing mattered. Everything felt meaningless after another nonconsensual interaction, except this time, I wasn't under. I was fully alert and still unable to defend myself against more unrighteous acts. Was I only worth my body? What about my heart? Did no one see that? There I was in that dark room. All by myself. No one understood why I was so cold and isolated. I blamed myself. I hated everyone. All I could do was indulge and be under.

Another couple of months went by and I met Guel. After that ended, I had to ask myself "is this the path you want to go down again? Will you allow yourself to get that low every time someone hurts you? Will you keep letting people who hurt you determine your fate?" No! I had to tell myself I will no longer allow this. Although staying in that room and closing the door was much easier than trying to fix the light after all of the damage, it was worth it in the end.

Chapter 3: Power

Only you have the power to fix yourself. Only you have the power to make the change. After meeting Guel, he wanted to change me. Wanted me to forget my past and move on like nothing happened. We cannot run from our past. We must face it head on. We must close a chapter to start a new one. I did not need answers. I needed to process how this all affected me. Giving Guel the power to determine how my days went would only allow more disappointment. We think that someone can come along and replace our fix. If we allow that, if things get ugly with your new fix, or the new fix is no longer there, we will resort to our old ways. The childhood friend was the first fix. After becoming involved with him, I stopped it all... for him. No more containers, no more bottles, no more needing to be fixed. But he was just a bandage on a wound that needed to be stitched.

When that bandage was ripped off, the only stitching that was there was the poison fueling me... so it seemed. This was only a pain relief to the unstitched wound.

We must change for ourselves. Then, no person or problem can determine how we make decisions. We cannot be sorry while we wait for the next fix. We must be our own fix. After Guel, there could not be another downfall. I was being put into a box and believing that I should go for all of the mistreatment. This is what I deserved right? No, wrong. We must have the power to let people walk out the door when they want to shut the door to our room. We must let them leave when they want to turn off our real light, bring their own, and make us believe that we cannot shine without them.

How can I take my power back? I must believe that I can. I must want to. While in the process, it may seem impossible. It is not. It can be done. Giving yourself the power to walk away is the key to change. This can be eliminating a person, substance, mindset, or even a lethargic lifestyle. We must sit ourselves down and ask ourselves "is this the pain I want to keep allowing myself to endure? Do I want to wake up everyday and wish I didn't?" No one wants to feel sorrowful, regretful, and miserable. We do not have to mourn the life we wish we had. We can create it. It is never too late. We are our own time machine. We decide when to start over, move forward, and change our ways. Can people help you through this process? Of course they can. But you... you must be the determining factor. Never give someone else the power to dictate your life. If we want difference, we must stop allowing people to walk over and corner us in a position that only gives us room for a downfall. There is so much more to achieve. Being in that room, I only looked outside of the door and saw the lights on in other people's rooms. I never looked outside the window to see myself smiling and living a different life. Turn the light on. Open the window. See things from a different angle.

Overcoming

Chapter 4: Sorrow

When we are fighting battles between our mind and our heart, we can get lost in the process. We can fall into a state of sorrow or dependence. We can be sorry and wish we went about things differently. But all we can do is wish for those things, because we cannot change the past. Being awake but unable to get out of the bed.

Being awake but unable to get anything done. Being awake and doing our best to sleep the day away. Being awake and unable to accomplish anything. Those are all traits of sorrow. It is okay to feel and cry. But how long can we allow ourselves to stay in this state? How long can we keep the lights off in our room before we keep falling off the bed? How long will we allow ourselves to get bruises from falling? How long will we allow someone else to break the light so that we cannot turn it back on? We must stand up. Stand up and say enough is enough.

It is expected to feel the way we feel, process, and recover. Each step of the way will take a different amount of time for each person. We are not allocated a specific number of minutes or hours to feel. Still, we must tell ourselves when it is time to start this process and recover. I never told myself that. I let myself fall off the bed so loudly, it woke up everyone in the rooms around me. "Just turn on the light!" It wasn't that easy. I could no longer reach the light. I knew it was there, but I was not strong enough to flip the switch. Looking in from the outside, everyone wondered why someone with such a beautiful door keeps the lights off in the room.

They'd try to turn that light on, when only I had the power to do so. Only I could reverse the darkness. Some wanted me myself to turn that light on, some wanted to turn the light on for me, and some wanted to bring in their own light so that when I had the strength to turn mine on, they would turn it back off and say I only needed their light. To say I must depend on them to shine. Was I nothing without them? Did I need them? Falling into that trap will never give you incentive to move forward.

No person holds your light. It is better to allow yourself to feel and heal, than allow someone else to determine that for you. Allowing someone else to have that light, and giving them the batteries to fix their light prevented me from turning on my own light. During that time of giving someone else the power to fix me, I was not learning how to fix myself. I was counting on them to turn on the lights every morning. I must create my own groove. Tell myself good morning. Tell myself goodnight. Tell myself "I love you."

We are allowed to grieve the loss of a tie with someone. We must not stay down. Time is the most important part of healing. There is no set amount of time needed to heal. But what is the difference between healing and isolation? It was quite easy to shut that door once Guel left. But this time... it was time for something different. It was time to go through the process to get that light working again. That light is happiness. That light is motivation. That light is self love.

Some sorrows are ordinary. Others are not. When you have already experienced a battle with indulgence and despair, it can easily worsen when someone comes along, fixes you, and disappears. Do not allow mistreatment. Do not stay until you hate them. Do not put yourself through pain because you do not want to hurt someone else. Do not allow yourself to turn off your light because it is brighter than someone else's. One of the biggest problems when battling sorrow is believing that you are so hard to deal with that you should allow someone to mistreat you. If someone is not fit to care for your excessive need for reassurance and comfort, leave. If someone is mistreating you and suggesting it is because of your mental health, leave.

This is manipulation for you to think "no one else will stay through my battles." I was taught a lot during that time with Guel. I was taught to love myself. The whole time I thought I was given the one, when I was actually given a lesson. A lesson as to why

I should never let someone make me believe that my light could never be turned on. A lesson as to why my light will always be the brightest in my room. No one else's light can replace your own.

After the batteries in that light stopped working again, I did not bother to replace them. I did not bother to find a new light. It was time to let my own light shine. My light is not powered by batteries or what I have to offer. My light is powered by my mind and heart. All I needed was self love. Although the light would still occasionally go off, I now had the power to turn it back on. Now that the brightness of my light was in my hands, I was the determining factor in my life.

Wow! Now what? I'd gotten so used to someone else determining my happiness I didn't even know where to start. What do I do when my light is off? Who will be there to turn it back on? Now it was time for me to put myself first. It was time for me to do the work and recover from the stampede that took place in that dark room. After wondering if I just was not loveable, I began to love myself again. I began to smile. The light was starting to work sometimes. But now that everything is better, why doesn't the light always work? Was I still doing something wrong? No. I wasn't doing anything wrong. Instead of someone else being the cause of my sorrow, it was up to me now. While the sorrows might still be present after the absence of a tie, I only had myself to work on. I did not have to try and fix a relationship that was never really there. I only needed to make change within.

That was a big only though. How can I do this all by myself? Some people are able to move forward and heal without a helping hand. Others need to seek additional help from a parent, or even professionally. That is okay. It is okay to ask for help. The goal is to get better, not isolate yourself and hope that you heal. Isolation can be a huge enemy, especially when you have been hurt and don't know how to trust. Trust is something that is earned, however we should not shut down every hand that is offered. We do not want to become bitter in the process. Some people commend themselves for shutting out the world and becoming emotionless. I tried that and realized that is not what I wanted for myself. There is absolutely nothing wrong with wanting to live alone, have no kids, or not get married. But personally, I did not want that. I knew that I wanted to get married and have a family someday. So I had to begin healing so that when someone did come along, I was able to love them correctly. It still takes time. After battling sorrow, indulgence, worry, or any other illness, you should heal. Heal first, love yourself, then bring someone into your life. You do not want to give someone the light switch to your lights. If they try to take it with them or leave, you will not know how to be self-sufficient. You will not have done the work to become something great. It is important to love yourself before loving someone else. If you only allow love from the outside, you will not hold love within.

Chapter 5:
Dependence

Oh that feels good. The feeling of being under. Not worrying about your emotions. One more time won't hurt. That is what we tell ourselves when we are continuously indulging. We keep doing that and do not realize how lost we are becoming. How many emotions and how much trauma we are suppressing, until it all blows up in your face. 287 days. That's how many days I would have been abstinent if I stopped the day it all came to head. The day Guel begged me to never pick it up again. That day, I said "okay, I am done. I will never pick it up again." Is it possible to stop cold turkey? Yes, anything is possible. But was that the right way to approach the situation? All of the suppressed feelings were coming out. The tears were flowing, the nightmares were recurring, and the feelings of worthlessness were showing more than ever. So what did I do? I picked it up again, and again, and again. I hadn't done the work to heal. I was only using poison to fuel myself. It was time to do some damage control. Process all of the things that happened last summer. Processing? That didn't feel too good. So what did I do? I picked it up again. Seeing the tears in Guel's eyes. That hurt me. I stopped. No more picking it up.

Then, Guel started being cold. But why was he being so cold? I did what he asked. I switched my dependence from indulgence to him. He was my new fix. He made me feel better. He made me happy. He made me smile. He brought me light. But he started taking his light back. So what did I do? I picked it up again. Not because of Guel. But because Guel was only distracting me from the many things I'd already gone through. But once Guel finally turned that light off for good, I was left in that dark room. But now I didn't even want to indulge. I wanted to turn my own light on.

I had to take a step back. Why did I ever start indulging? What part of me needed healing? I needed to overcome my past. I needed to take a deep look into every event that led me here. Why would I want to be under if being under got me into disturbing circumstances? In hopes of forgetting that night, I kept indulging and indulging and indulging. Keeping it all to myself. Never talking about it. Then there was a pause. I met someone. Then there was a replay. He was gone. Then I took indulging to a new level. Waking up to get some poison. That poison felt so good I didn't recognize it was poison. That is where the dependence started. I never got the chance to mourn the loss of a tie I deemed so special. So when I finally decided to stop, a year's worth of trauma was thrown at me all at once. During the five months of heavy indulgence, I never had the chance to heal. I was not coming face to face with anything. I was instead locking myself in that room and pushing everything under the door as I took a sip.

It is mandatory to overcome each situation as it comes to you. Bottling it up and trying to forget about it is only a temporary aid. While it may be difficult, we must process and take our power back. We cannot stay in that room forever. It is about when and how we come out of it. The longer we wait, the more demons we allow to creep in. The more pain we allow ourselves to endure, the more pressure we put on ourselves trying to suppress reality. There is a difference between an occasional glass after a stressful day and going completely under and spoiling our dependence. I gave in. I completely gave in. I gave up on myself. I did not think I would ever get better. I did not see a purpose in bothering to try, because I knew I would always feel this way... so I thought. There is so much more to life than a relationship. There is so much more to life than the need for someone to love you. Love yourself. If you love yourself and someone wants to walk out of your life, you will not have to question your value. You will already know that you are worth loving. You will already know that you have value. We must not switch or turn off our dependence for anyone but for ourselves. This was my world. This was my life. Why would I let someone determine whether or not I am happy? Why would I give someone else the power to dictate my emotions and my struggles? Eventually, I realized there was more to life than sitting around mourning the life I thought I'd have. That is how I turned that light back on. That is how I took the black out curtains off the window in that room. I was depending on someone else to take me out of my misery. I should have been depending on myself. You should be depending on yourself. Do not let anyone ever make you feel like you need them to survive. That is an unhealthy way of living. Dependence does not have to be on a drug. It can be on a person. Both are the wrong approach.

Create a routine. Create a way to get out of that room. It is a process. We must process the underlying cause of our dependence before we focus on the dependence itself. Is it trauma? Is it a mental health disorder? What is it? We must first answer that question to start our journey of recovery. Processing these things hurts like a bitch. But processing them will allow us to open that door. Processing will allow us to cope. And it takes time. Months, years even. But at the end, you will thank yourself.

I needed closure. Not closure as, "why don't you want to stay?" But closure as, "how can I close that chapter of my life in order to move on and be successful?"

Chapter 6:
Recurrence

What is recurrence? What makes something recurrent? Recurrence is the repetitive action or occurrence of something; when something happens repetitively.

I'd moved on from the first problem. Things are getting better... right? Well why am I still sad? Why do I still feel like this? Those questions remained unanswered. I turned my head in the opposite direction. I did not know answering those questions would put me ten steps ahead. So what did I do? I picked it up AGAIN. I was set twenty steps back. I was doing it all over again. The original goal was to stop. But what does that mean? What does abstinence mean? It means cutting all ties with your dependence. It is okay to take your time. This process looks different for everyone. I did not know that I should lessen my intake slowly until I was no longer dependent. That was what worked for me. Choosing when I would indulge rather than doing it everyday. I found it was better to do it when my body wasn't fiending the most, because when it was, I would overindulge. While I wish I'd never picked it up to begin with, there was no going back.

What does rock bottom look like? Rock bottom looks different for everyone. Some could say I was far from it. Others could say I was at the lowest of the low. I had my share of indulgences for about four years before I actually hit rock bottom. I hadn't taken the time to heal, so for many months after my heart was broken, I'd indulge. Not an indulgence you take when you're out with your friends. An indulgence you take when you don't want to feel. When you want to sleep and be in your own zone. By the time I was ready to turn my life around, I was so far deep I didn't know what to do. This time it wasn't about turning a light on in a room. It was about kicking out a negative spirit. A spirit that moved into the room and was there to stay. When the lights were on, it was still there, just less visible. But when the lights were off, that spirit would try to suffocate me. It was time for me to breathe. Sounds easy right? Wrong. That spirit would not just disappear. It was to be evicted.

For five months, the spirits were in my room everyday. There would be an occasional day where the spirit would sleep, but the lights still weren't on. Now, there was a dark room with a demonic spirit. A spirit of hatred. A spirit of misery. Would it talk to me today? I didn't know until I woke up. But for 150 days, that spirit was talking to me. That spirit was feeding me poison telling me it would make me feel better. And it did... temporarily. The road to recovery is not a straight path. It is a path with many curves and maybe even detours. After those long five months, I began the path. That lasted about a month. Then I took a detour. That detour was only for a day. Then I found the right path again. I was breathing. I was removing the blanket put on me by that spirit. I hadn't gotten my light to work yet, so I was following a dark path. It seemed so easy to follow a path that was straight. What I didn't know was at the end of that straight path, was another container. What I also didn't know was that the detours would lead me to the same ending as the straight path. Point is, the path that seems easiest may not be the right path. It is there as an escape from the right path. It was there as an easy way out of the long road to recovery.

It is okay to have setbacks. But we must not allow that spirit to control us again. We must evict that spirit. At first, it will try and come back, but eventually it will get the point. We must understand that we can still take the right path, even if we end up on a negative detour. Why give up hope? Why not keep going? It seemed so hard at the time. By the time I was near the end of the long, curvy path, I did not want to go back again. I did not want to pick it up. Some may even have an occasional indulgence. That is better than going under and staying under. If we cannot cut the ties with the spirit, we must have a healthy relationship with it. We must know the difference.

Well, what is the difference? The difference is indulging for the body rather than the mind. If we are using it not to feel, we will never want to feel again. And when we do feel, we will resort back to our dependence. When we do it when we are in a decent state of mind, our negative thoughts will not return once we are lucid again.

When will you stop allowing recurrence of sorrow and dependence? When will you evict those spirits and turn the lights back on?

Chapter 7:
Recollection

When you are lucid you are able to feel. These feelings are not necessarily bad feelings. You are able to recall both pleasant memories and unpleasant trauma. When we grieve the loss of a tie, we are grieving the loss of the pleasant memories. We wonder what we could have done to make those memories continue. We must recognize that if those memories outweighed the pain, we would still be making them. If two people grow apart that is one thing. But when someone is breathing in manipulative air, they will eventually suffocate. Those spirits are not the only thing that can suffocate you. Toxic air can too. We must clean out the air filter in order to breathe properly. We must remove those manipulators from our lives. We cannot blame ourselves for the actions of others. Looking back on the beautiful moments does not show the stress we endured. Every tie has its troubles. But some troubles are not worth it. Not worth your happiness, and certainly not worth your sanity.

When I think about the laughs I had with Guel and the way my face lit up, the troubles are not present. But when I recall why it ended, they are. When I recall the late night worries about why I wasn't enough, I know that I never want to feel that way again. I know that I never want to have to second guess whether or not I am worth loving. When the bads and goods are put together, I let them cancel each other out. Whether they were 50:50, 60:40, or even 51:49, I remember that when I put them together they equal 100. A whole. When I think about that chapter of my life, I see how much I have grown since then. How far I have come. And I say to myself, if someone cannot help me fix my own light, I do not need theirs to distract me from fixing my own. It is okay to miss it. It is okay to wish things were different. It is not okay to allow yourself to undo all of your progress for a potential love story. Never let someone show you that they do not want you more than once. Never let someone tell you that your light can never be turned on. Prove them wrong. Show them that their light was only so dull, they had no idea how bright a light could get. No idea how many positive spirits could live in your room.

We also have unpleasant memories and trauma. We must learn from our past. Reflect on it rather than dwell on it. Learn how to trust. Learn how to love without depending on someone. When I think of that night, I realize how many things could have gone dfferently. What if I didn't indulge? What if he wasn't there? What if he respected my boundaries? Those are all what ifs. Although I stayed in a state of indulgence for a while after that, I learned. I learned not to put myself in such a vulnerable situation. I learned to separate my social life and my mental battles. Although this led to the choosing of indulgence over friendships, it kept me safe. Create a plan. What will you do if you are in a certain situation? What can you do dfferently next time? Although the actions of others have no dependence on you, what will you do if someone decides to cross a boundary you have set?

We must feel. Feeling is the only way to recover. We must recall the events that brought us here. We must find closure in the things we were unable to control. We must process and decide what to do next. I waited so long to do that. Now, I have the constant battle of what to do when I feel. I went so long without feeling, feeling seems so foreign to me. Why must I feel? To be aware. To understand myself. I realized that every time I felt an unpleasant emotion, I would indulge. We must allow ourselves to go through the process of remembering and healing. It is difficult at first. Once we find closure and move past each event, we will be putting ourselves ten steps ahead. Suppressing these emotions will only cause an overwhelming feeling that can lead to more indulging. It will become a never ending cycle. Either we can allow a build up of hatred, sorrow, and misery while we indulge to forget, or we process, heal, and move forward.

Chapter 8:
Prosperity

The only way to prosper is to heal. We must heal ourselves before becoming involved with someone else. Would you invite someone in your room with the light off? I wouldn't. How would they see? Do you want them to trip and fall with you? Some people use others to turn their own lights on. Guel did this to me. His light was turned off by someone that was previously in the room. My light was turned off by the spirit of dependence. I was only to work on myself. I needed to heal my mind from myself. He needed to fix a room that was wrecked by someone else. There was a difference. I was no longer searching for answers. I was wanting to move forward with someone by my side. He was looking for answers that he could not get from someone else. While I was there to fill a void, he was there to teach me a lesson.

I knew why my room was dark, but he didn't know why his was. I knew that I needed to work on myself. While I thought I was building something great with him, he used me as a way to overcome his dependence on who was in his room. Had I loved myself and realized my worth, I would have never allowed him to manipulate me and constantly overlook my feelings. I would have recognized the work that needed to be done before our connection. Although we both had work to do, he was trying to replace one dependence with another. I was trying to overcome my dependence in general.

You want to be mentally solid before adding a new element to your life. If not, things will become chaotic. That time with

Guel was very chaotic. He often projected his past spirits into my room. I could not project mine, because mine did not come from a person. There were so many aspects that withheld me from prosperity. Sorrow. Trauma. Dependence.

To overcome the dependence, I had to look at the causes of it, which were sorrow and trauma. The sorrow came from within. There was no cause for the sorrow, only a cause for it worsening. The trauma came from one night, one day, then being abandoned. I had to get love from myself. I had to get up without depending on someone or something else to lead me to do so. The sorrow became so prevalent I did not want to get out of the bed. I did not want to eat. I did not want to do anything. I was losing myself. The things I used to love to do became so bothersome. I hated everything. Once I evicted the spirit and turned on the light, I saw that I needed to do things for myself. Dress nice for myself. Go out by myself. Take myself out to eat. Spend time learning and understanding myself.

After spending time connecting with myself, I learned that I do need time to be alone. I cannot spend every minute of the day around someone else. I must take time to let out the negative spirits, let in the positive spirits, and check on my light. In essence, I needed to have a heart-to-heart with myself. I needed to understand what triggered the sorrow and worry. This allowed me to recognize when to eliminate myself from an environment. Whether this was a social setting, a chaotic environment, or even taking a break from studying or working.

Some live for the thrill. Some live for the adrenaline rush. Some live for peace. I thought I was living for the thrill. Maybe I was before. But now, I need peace of mind and tranquility. I don't like for my mind to be running in different directions. I like to be focused. Being focused led me to do better things in life. Being focused led me on a path to start my career. Being focused led me to become closer to those I love. Tranquility and focus is how I was able to prosper. Once I turned on the lights and let that negative spirit out, I was able to look out of the window and see that I needed to leave the room. I could still come back to it, but I needed to see more. Try new things. Free my mind.

Chapter 9: Reversal

With the road to recovery comes doubts and temptations. After years of sorrow I believed that my light would never stay on. When I was finally working on fixing that light, it was easier to leave it how it was. I found comfort in that dark room. It was all I knew. What would it look like when that light was finally on? We must not live in fear. We must do our best to eliminate what is causing our light not to work. We must eliminate the magnet that was attracting those negative spirits. We must eliminate those who are telling us their light is all we need and to never fix our own. Once we go through the process of elimination, we will be able to make change. We can mourn the loss of those we lost in the process, but we must also remember why they were to be eliminated. This is not a smooth road. Every door wants to be the best door, and every room wants to shine the brightest. We cannot allow ourselves to dwell on what could have been. We must focus on what can be and what will be. I had to ask myself, "Is relighting a flame I did not blow out worth resetting all of my progress?" When I did not believe it was possible to move forward, I decided it was at least worth trying. What were the options? Try and fail, try and succeed, and don't try and stay in this state of despair.

After beginning abstinence, temptations were quite abundant. If I was sorrowful, should I take the easy route and indulge, or should I start the process of recovery? If I was fiending, should I indulge or should I start the process of recovery? Even after 30 days of no contact, I still had the desire. The dependence hadn't fully subsided. 35 days after beginning that road to recovery, I took a detour. It was a small detour, but it was still a detour. Then, I got back on the right path. Soon after, I took another detour. One detour led to two detours, two led to three, and the cycle restarted. Now, I was again under the spell of the spirit of dependence. How could I overcome this? Rather than beginning with abstinence, I decided to discipline myself. Some days I would talk to the spirit. Some days, I would turn that light on. Some days, I would position myself to breathe from under the blanket that was suffocating me. If I couldn't go from all to nothing, I could go from all to something. I could slowly create ways to eliminate that dependence from my routine.

During that time, I wanted to give up. During that time, I lost friends. During that time, I had people telling me I'd never get better. But I didn't do it for them. I didn't do it to rekindle the relationships I lost. I did it for myself. I did it because I saw my potential. Every time I took a detour, I said it was the last time. It was never the last time. It was now about how far I'd get in between each detour. That was what mattered. That was now the determining factor. There was only one road this time. Except, I was right in the middle. To the left was comfort, indulgence, forgetfulness, and carelessness, but one hundred miles down was a dark hole, which made the road back to the middle twice as long. To the right was sorrow, despair, feelings, but if I made it through the uncomfortable 100 miles, there was a pot of gold at the end. This dark hole was dependence. This dark hole was losing myself. This dark hole was the walls caving in on me. And the pot of gold... don't you want to know what was in the pot of gold? In that pot was joy. In that pot was prosperity. In that pot was quality of life.

I was keeping my lights off for comfort. It was easier to sleep in the dark when I was under. With the lights off, I did not pay attention to the spirits that were attracted to that darkness. I did not recognize the spirits I was letting into my room. I was comfortable. I eventually learned how to see in the dark. When the light was on, it was so bright. I hadn't seen that light in so long it nearly blinded me. So what did I do? I closed my eyes until the light went off again.

After months of turning the light on and off, letting the spirit in and evicting it again, I fell back under the spell. Except now, I'd incorporated my dependence into my routine. Instead of fully submerging myself under the waters, I stayed in the shallow parts. Just enough to keep the spirits there, but not enough to fully drown... so I thought. I was still drowning, but this time I was holding my own head under the water. There wasn't just a sudden flood in that dark room. There was a little bit of water filling the room by the day. And eventually, I drowned.

I wasn't starting over. There is no starting over. When we tell ourselves we are putting our past behind us and starting over, that is not actually what we are doing. Our past will always subconsciously affect how we make decisions. Our past will either teach us or hold us back. We will either live in fear or learn ourselves and learn how to adapt. That's it! I was learning how to adapt. But not in a positive way. I was learning how to breathe with water in my lungs. I taught myself how to see in the dark. Those were the adaptations I made, when I should have been learning how to swim and fix the light.

Every time we take a detour, we are only elongating our path. We are not getting a new path and starting over. Some will be able to immediately follow the path to the end. Others will not. No matter how many times we turn around, go backwards, or take a detour, we are still on the same path. It is the journey of life. It is okay to take a detour, as long as you are learning in the process. As long as you are aware you are doing so. Being aware goes a long way. It is when we are in denial that we are unable to start this journey. When we are saying, "I don't have a problem. I can stop whenever I want," knowing that is far from the truth. Your road to recovery will not look like the roads of others. Mine sure didn't. My road had a four way stop sign every mile. At these stop signs were different ways to escape this road and go back into that room. While being on this road trip, I was allowing time for renovations in the room. I was allowing God to go into that room and give it a makeover. Turn the light on. Pray the spirits away.

One of the biggest benefits of this road is it being your road. This was my road. I could walk as slow as I wanted down this road. I had a goal for myself. These detours and recurrences were not necessarily setting me back. That was only one way to look at it. They were building me a better road to walk on. Now that I was aware of the problem, I was able to create my own solutions. I was able to recognize what could be done differently. That is progress. No one can tell you whether or not you are making progress. You must know. Yes, people can commend you along the way, but only you know how far you are really coming. Yes, people can criticize you, but only you know how much progress you have made.

These reversals and setbacks do not have to be looked at as such. Look at this as part of the process. When learning, we may make the same mistake several times before truly understanding what needs to be done. That... that means we are truly learning. We can go through the motions and recover, but we want to also learn during the process. We want to be able to help ourselves grow. Recovering and becoming abstinent is not the only thing in that pot of gold. Knowledge and growth are in it as well.

Destiny: The predetermined creation of how life will be

Chapter 10: Love

When we say the words "I love you" we are expressing intense feelings. When we love someone romantically we want to be with them forever. But what does this look like? What if the person we love doesn't love us back? What if the person we love doesn't love us enough to make change? What if the person we love is treating us so poorly, but we stay because we love them? In my case, those were not what ifs, those were realities. My realities. There are different types of love. Love with an emotional connection. Love with a soul tie from intimate interactions. And love out of fear of abandonment.

When we create a tie with someone out of pure emotions and connections, that is love. When we connect with someone and tell them everything. When we feel like we cannot live without them. When they hold a piece of our heart. That is how I felt. But why did I feel this way? He didn't. How could I still have these feelings of love when I was being treated so poorly? How could I feel this way about someone who disrespects me? Who yells at me and calls me a "bitch?" How? Because the love was already there. The more I felt that love, the more I realized how hurt I would be if it ever ended. And it did. Some people stay until they are out of love. Until they hate that person. I did not want to do that. When I became lucid and understood that loyalty and respect should come first, I was able to walk away. Do not let someone trample you because you love them. You may not want to walk away, because you don't want to hurt them. Love yourself more. Love yourself more than you could possibly love anyone else. Just because we feel deep affection for someone does not mean we have to spend the rest of our lives with them. When we feel that drift, we must take a step back and look. Look at what caused the drift. Look at whether or not it was a drift or a disconnection by the other person. More often than not we want to fix something that we did not break. We want to relight a flame on a candle that we did not blow out. Sometimes we create a destiny in our own mind. If I love someone then I should just be with them right? Even if they treat me like shit? Even if they make me feel like I don't matter? Who else will I love? No. No. No. Do not stay with someone just because you love them. Stay because y'all love each other and are able to respect each other, be loyal to one another. Being loyal isn't just staying out of bed with everyone except your person. Being loyal is protecting your person's name. Showing those who speak against your person that you stand with your person. Being loyal is choosing your person. Being loyal is never making your person an option. That is loyalty. Respecting your person isn't just not calling them out of their name. Respecting them is taking the time to listen. Taking the time to understand. And taking the time to hear them.

Just because we once thought someone was the one for us doesn't mean we can't change our minds. It doesn't mean it is set in stone. By staying in these manipulative situations we are degrading ourselves. We are showing ourselves that we are only worth the bare minimum. Be worth more. I know I am. I know that I deserve someone who will sit down and listen to my fears, thoughts, and emotions. I know I deserve someone who will do their best to understand me rather than starting a dispute and going into defense mode. Know your worth. No one can set your value. Set your own. Be true to yourself, and put yourself first.

Chapter 11: Life

"When I grow up I want to be a doctor!" "When I grow up I want to be a firefighter!" "When I grow up I want to be a pilot!" We have all said this before. At such a young age we wanted to create our story. It was cute as a kid, but now... now we must reread that story. We must make changes to best suit our current lifestyle. Ever since I could remember, I wanted to follow the traditional lifestyle: go through grade school, graduate, go to college, graduate, and get a job. I never added the in between and possibilities of change. I thought that was the right thing to do. In reality, only YOU can make you successful. You are writing your own story. We did not WRITE our story. We are WRITING our story. We are writing it as we go, and we can make as many changes as we want. Just because we created our destinies in our head, we do not have to follow them. We can kick whoever we want out of our lives. We can make whatever changes we want. We can eliminate, we can add, and we can add as many pages as we want to our story.

We do not have to follow tradition. We can give ourselves a break. Whether that be a week off work to clear our minds. Whether it be a year out of school before starting a job or continuing to study. We write our own lives. No one can write it for us, and no one can tell us how to write it. We can erase or use a pen and draw a line through it. We can write in cursive. We can write in print. We can write in ALL CAPS IF WE WANT TO. We can use profanity. We can do whatever the fuck we want. This is our life. If we want to write it on a piece of paper or if we want to write it on a bunch of sticky notes. We can use complete sentences. We can use proper punctuation: or not. We CAN do whatever we want.

There does not have to be a reason for us to want to do what we do. Stop letting the traditions and goals of other people influence how you make decisions. Stop giving the pen to someone else to write your story. Even if you are halfway through your story, you can have a complete turn around and do something that does not in any way go with your previous decisions. If you think you may want to become a surgeon, go to med school. If you come out of med school and decide to become a teacher, then become a teacher.

Have you heard the term "It's just part of life?" Well this is part of life. Making changes and recreating your story is part of life. Although we cannot go back and reverse the steps we have already taken, we can walk in a different direction. We can even run. Who's to say you can't drop out of med school and start a fashion line? And if that fashion line is not something you wish to keep doing, and you want to go back to med school, then you can. There is no allocation of how many times you can change your mind. If there was, I would not have had the opportunity to be redirected and could have had a detrimental turn of events. Change your mind. Make the move. Be the change.

Chapter 12: Regret

Once we make a decision, we cannot undo it. We will forever live with the decisions we make. We have a choice. We can either live in regret or learn from our past decisions and experiences. We cannot always predict how our decisions will affect us later in life. We cannot predict the decisions others will make and how their decisions will affect us. We can only live in the present. We can only move forward. Every second you spend regretting the past, is a second you lose learning from it. Every second you spend trying to change the past, is a second you lose moving forward. We must learn, evolve, and elevate. We must use the story we cannot rewrite to write the next one. We must create an addition to our story. There are always several decisions to be made at each step of the way. Each decision made at step one, two, and three, can be used to make the next decision. It is okay to wish you did something different. It is not okay to spend countless hours regretting what was done. Instead, use that time to reflect and learn. There are so many opportunities in life. If the flood in the room led to water damage to the light, work on draining that water and repairing that light. Do not sit there wondering how you let the water in to damage your light. Do not sit there wondering if the light had been on, would there have been a desire to protect it from the water. There would have been. But the light was off. You cannot change that.

After that night, I spent so many days wondering... "what if I didn't indulge?" "What if I spoke up sooner?" After Guel I wondered, " what if I didn't let him into that room?" When I first began the road to recovery I wondered, "what if I never picked it up?" What if... what if things were different? Then, the story you are writing would be too. But it's not. It happened.

What did I learn? I learned to be mindful of how giving someone several chances to destroy me caused myself more detriment in the long run. I learned to stop hiding from my truth. I learned to love myself more than anyone else could ever love me. Possessing self love and acknowledging your truth will help you out of the hole of regret. It will shine light in that dark hole. It will show you the ladder you were unable to see in the dark. Regret... regret will show you a deeper path into the darkness. It will tell you that you are going up, when you are actually going down. It will toss you around like an undertow and cause you not to know which way is up and which way is down.

You do not have to commend yourself for the mistakes you made, but regret is no better than commending yourself for that mistake. Regret blocks the opportunity of learning. It blocks the opportunity for growth. It blocks the opportunity for self love.

Chapter 13: Contemplation

When we go through trauma, sorrow, regret, and dependence, we may not know just how to process the emotions we are feeling. Sometimes it seems like the easiest way out is to cross the bridge of life. At least for me it did. What worth did I have? Was I only here for people to use and destroy me? For people to talk down on my name? Was I only here to help others overcome their own battles? Did no one see me? Did no one see the battles I was fighting? Those were the questions I asked myself when I wanted to give up. I was so ready to put things to rest. But I didn't. I kept fighting. Was I just prolonging it to keep going through these emotions over and over again? No. I wasn't fighting hard enough. I was only fighting to stay here, not fighting to get better. I was not realizing how important life itself was. That light being off, those spirits in the room, the trauma, the pain, they were all a test. A test to see how much pain I could endure before I started my journey.

Do not wait until you are at the edge of the cliff. Do not allow yourself to walk towards that cliff. Do not put yourself in a position to fall off of the edge. Put on some better shoes. Put on some shoes that will keep you from continuously sliding closer to that edge. Stop yourself in your tracks and think. Think about the pain you are enduring. Put an end to it in a positive way. Do not break the light, fix it. You only get one light. Cherish that light. Make that light shine. Do not allow the water to rise so high that it permanently damages your light and causes it to flicker.

If you can't do it for yourself now, do it for those you love. Do it for those who love you. Do it for your future self. Do not squander your time wondering what the world would be like without you. If you think you don't make much of a difference now, then make a difference. Create more. We must not do things for the satisfaction of others, but for the satisfaction of ourselves.

Before making a decision so poor that you will never get to finish your story, skip a page in the book. Set some goals. If you have a goal, but do not know how to achieve it, write down what achievement looks like. And as you write that down, the steps needed to get there will come to you. As you write that down, God will fill out the rest of the page. You may feel alone now, but you are not. You have your mind. Your body. Your spirit. And most importantly, God. God is there when no one else is. God is the one who is making it difficult for you to cross that bridge of life. When he sees you trying to cross that bridge, he loosens its supports. God... God is why you haven't done it. God is why you are still here. So next time you think about crossing that bridge, ask him "Is this what you would do?" His answer will be no.

I know we write our own story, but God is there, and he is there to support us. To stand by our side. To tell us that we can do it. That you can do it. Do not burn your book just because you do not know what to write next. Skip a page. Go back and fill that part out later. The saying is for God to answer your prayers. But some prayers are not prayers. Praying for someone else to make you cross that bridge, is not a prayer. It is communication with the negative spirits. It is giving those spirits the okay to creep into your room. It is giving them the exact location of your room. So pray. Pray that God will remove those spirits from your room. Pray that God gives you the will to move on. Pray that God will revoke your right to talk to those spirits.

Pray with me:

Dear God,

I ask you for forgiveness of my sins. I ask you to release the demonic spirits from me. I ask you to take my hand and walk with me down my road to recovery. I ask you to give me the faith and the power to never say aloud again that I wish to take the life you have given me. I thank you for opening my eyes everyday. I thank you for bringing me this far. And I thank you in advance for staying by my side.

In Jesus' name, I ask and pray,
Amen.

Chapter 14: Realization

Now... now that you have prayed away those spirits. Now that you have given yourself the power by God, you realize just how far you have come. No one is able to understand the way your mind flows but you. No one is able to tell you that you have yet to grow. Hold that power. When you hold that power, when you are being told you have made no progress, or that you are progressing too slow, that negative energy will be redirected by the wind, by God. When you are breathing in that fresh air, it feels so good.

Praying those spirits away, draining that water, removing that blanket of suffocation, and turning my light back on was the best thing I ever did. I never thought I would be able to come this far. I never thought I would be able to recover. As I approached that pot of gold, I knew that I never wanted to go back to that dark hole. I was able to recognize and realize when I was letting those spirits in. I was able to understand why those spirits were ever able to creep into my room. I was able to know what to do when my light got dull.

I realize how many things would have been destroyed had I crossed that bridge. My family would have been heartbroken, lost, and left with no answers. They would have spent the rest of their lives living in sorrow and regret, wondering what they could have done differently. Wondering why I never reached out. Wondering why they never knew how much I was dealing with. We often conceal our battles so well that our door is shining, but our room is dark. We walk around with a smile on our face, yet hold so much pain in our heart. That is why no one saw my battles. Why no one felt the need to ask me if I was okay. On the outside I was very successful and seemed so content with my life. But on the inside... on the inside I had years of sorrow, mistreatment, and dependence.

I thank myself for walking away from that bridge. I thank myself for evicting the negative spirits and letting them get lost in the wind. I thank myself for putting it down. So thank yourself. Thank yourself for being here. Thank yourself for every ounce of progress, no matter how small. It will all add up at the end. There I was years deep in sorrow and dependence, thinking that my life was over. Thinking that I'd never be able to fix my light. But here I am abstinent. Shining.

We often do not think things could be better, myself included. I did not see the point of continuously fighting. But I kept trying and trying. Fighting and fighting. Then, something changed. I had no desire to keep falling into bad habits. I had no desire to try to see in the dark. I wanted to see what was inside that pot of gold. I wanted to continue writing my story. I couldn't write on the lines in the dark. I was just writing words on top of other words. Sentences on top of other sentences. Stories on top of other stories. I needed clarity. I needed to understand myself and my story. I needed to reread my story. Go back and make changes to add the detours on the road. I needed to remove the roadblocks. And I did. I removed the roadblocks and added the detours to my story. I accounted for the potential detours farther down the road. Once I added the additional steps I needed to take, I was able to keep walking down the road. I was able to prepare myself for other potential detours.

Chapter 15: Recurrence

Recurrence is not only present in dependence. It is present in sorrow. It is present in manipulation. It is present in self doubt. Every time I put it down, I ended up picking it up again. After going through this seemingly never ending cycle, I managed to have longer breaks of abstinence. I remember very vividly the last time I wanted to pick it up, my dad came in my room that morning just to tell me he loved me. To give me a hug. He wanted nothing else. That day could be the reason I am still here. Who knows what would have happened had I picked it up again? He didn't know anything was wrong. He had no idea that I was feeling so low that day I wanted to indulge. Seeing the look of worry on my mom and little sister's face when they found me in my state of being under. Seeing the pain my family felt. The confusion. That is what kept me from crossing that bridge. I was right by the beginning of the bridge. I was holding the handles of it on both sides. But my feet had yet to step on it.

Every time the sorrow overpowers me, I must ask myself, what will I do about it? I found myself in a cycle where the sorrow caused indulgence. And the indulgence was a way of masking the pain so strong that I wanted to cross that bridge. The light was working now, but it kept flickering. I never knew when it would come back on. On that road to recovery there were so many helping hands. I'd never seen them, because I'd never gotten far enough. I was still near the middle of the road of recovery and the road to downfall. I could still see the emotionless, indulging me. I could still see the comfort I found in staying under that blanket. The comfort I found in breathing in that toxic air. The comfort I found in the dark. The comfort was blocking the dark hole. The discomfort at the beginning stage of recovery was blocking the pot of goal. I was leading myself in the wrong direction.

With the help of God and the power I have given myself, I have been able to move forward. That light still flickers due to water damage. But that is from decisions I made that I cannot change. That is from a me that no longer exists. I cannot live in regret of these decisions. I had to learn how to accommodate the flickering light. I had to know when to check on the wires that led to the shine. I had to do the work. Every time I feel the deep sorrow creeping back, I take power over it. In order for us to coexist, I must have the power. I learned to build a healthy relationship with sorrow and dependence. I learned that it was beyond my control at this point, but I could control my reaction to it. I can control it. I will control it. And I am controlling it. This control looks different for everyone. Some want to cut all ties with their dependence and are able to successfully do so. Others create a healthy relationship to understand how much to give in to these feelings and emotions.

The feelings come back. They are now part of us. Which is why we cannot get a new light. We must strengthen the one we have. We must reach out for more when we are ready to do the work and make the change. When I decided I was ready to make the change and fix my light, I was able to do so with additional help. However, I was the determining factor. I had to determine whether or not I would let myself get help. Whether or not I would reach out when I felt those spirits creeping back in. I had to unlock the door to that room to get in touch with myself. To allow myself to be heard. We choose which pages to add to our story. With the help and power of God, we can keep writing our story. So keep writing yours.

Lauren Reed is a passionate scholar, writer, and speaker dedicated to helping others overcome imposter syndrome and limited mindsets to achieve their full potential. Currently studying psychology at the Georgia Institute of Technology, Lauren is on a mission to become a psychiatrist and continue to help others on a deeper level.

With a keen interest in the human mind and behavior, Lauren has dedicated her studies and research to understanding how we can overcome mental barriers and limiting beliefs to lead happier, more fulfilling lives. Her work has been recognized for its impact and significance, and she has been invited to speak at various conferences and events to share her knowledge and experience.

Beyond her academic pursuits, Lauren is also an avid writer and blogger, where she shares her insights on personal growth and development. Her writing has been featured in various publications and platforms, and her work has inspired many to take action toward their goals and dreams.

Lauren lives in Atlanta with her loving family, including her mom and dad, baby sister London, and beloved dog Kody. When she's not studying or writing, Lauren enjoys spending time with her family, exploring new places, and trying out new recipes in the kitchen.

With her passion for helping others and her dedication to her craft, Lauren is a rising star in the field of psychology, and her work is sure to make a lasting impact on those she comes into contact with.